CW01213261

Original title:
Winter's Quiet Serenade

Copyright © 2024 Creative Arts Management OÜ
All rights reserved.

Author: Clara Whitfield
ISBN HARDBACK: 978-9916-94-570-4
ISBN PAPERBACK: 978-9916-94-571-1

Frostbitten Serenity's Song

In the chill, my nose turns red,
While snowflakes land right on my head.
My fingers dance, oh what a sight,
Just trying to keep warm while it's bright!

Whispers Beneath the Snow

Beneath the blanket, secrets lurk,
A mouse slips by, it's quite the perk.
Snowflakes chat like giddy friends,
While chilly winds play 'catch the bends'.

The trees wear coats, so dapper and neat,
But really, who knew snow could be sweet?
Frosty bunnies hop with flair,
Making snow angels in the air!

The Hush of Frozen Pines

Pines stand tall with snowy hats,
Dancing 'round like silly brats.
The owls chuckle, 'Who do we spy?'
While foxes somersault and fly!

Snowballs fling in a playful spree,
A secret pact between you and me.
Icicles laugh as they dangle low,
Wishing for socks to warm their toe!

Solitary Walks Through the Snow

I stroll alone, a frosty boss,
With every step, I fear I'll toss.
The snow it squeaks, sings in delight,
I wonder who'll join my snowball fight.

Ethereal Trails in Frozen Air

Footprints vanish, a magical thief,
Chasing squirrels, oh what a belief!
They scamper away, so quick and spry,
While I slip and slide, my cheeks go awry.

The Serenity of a Snow-Covered World

A blanket white, so fluffy and bright,
I giggle as I fall, oh what a fright!
The world's a canvas, my laughter does swirl,
In this frosty wonder, my joy does unfurl.

Silent Echoes of Frost

In the garden, silence reigns,
A snowman winks, but it's just plain.
Squirrels freeze mid-leap in time,
While penguins moonwalk, oh what a crime!

The mailbox creaks with frozen cheer,
As icicles drip, have no fear.
Snowflakes giggle upon my hat,
Saying, "Hey buddy, we like this spat!"

Chilling Lullabies of Night

The moon casts a glow on frozen lakes,
As penguins slide on their frosty quakes.
Rabbits hop and slip in glee,
Singing tunes of a snow-bound spree.

Hold tight your cocoa, don't let it spill,
As snowflakes whirl—what a thrill!
Lullabies croon through the pines,
Wishing on stars that love defines.

The Beauty of Absent Sound

Snowflakes dance, they tiptoe light,
Noses red, a comical sight.
Silence blankets the world in cheer,
As squirrels plot their nutty career.

Laughter echoes, but not a sound,
Just the crunching feet on the ground.
With every step, a slip in the mix,
Winter's laughter brings us new tricks.

Soft Embrace of a Frosty Fog

Frosty whispers creep and crawl,
Invisible hugs that tickle us all.
Mittens lost, the search is on,
Who knew a sock could be so drawn?

Fog rolls in, a massive prank,
Cocoa's warmth, our favorite tank.
Through the haze, a snowman grins,
He's got carrot dreams and happy sins.

Serene Icicles in Quiet Night

Icicles hang, they look like spears,
Guardians of the silent years.
They tremble too, when the wind starts,
A frozen symphony of tiny parts.

In the night, the world appears,
Snowflakes falling like giggling peers.
Nature's joke, it's all a tease,
We slip on ice, with grace, if you please.

A Shimmering Stillness Unfolds

A shimmer unfolds, frosty and bright,
Blankets of snow, a laugh at night.
Footprints trace a silly dance,
Snowballs fly, it's winter's chance.

Stillness reigns, but not for long,
A snowman wears my scarf – so wrong!
With each giggle, the cold grows bold,
A winter playground, stories told.

Surrender of the Autumn Leaves

The leaves are falling, what a sight,
They twirl and tumble, full of fright.
Once so proud, now they flee,
Surrendering to the barest tree.

A squirrel slips on a yellow sheet,
He scolds the breeze beneath his feet.
The ground is a carpet, crunching loud,
While birds are laughing, how absurdly proud!

Secret Stories in the Dark Chill

The moon is peeking, shivering low,
She whispers tales of ice and snow.
A rabbit wearing socks of blue,
Stands guard, reporting to the crew.

Icicles hanging like frozen spears,
Eavesdrop on secrets, despite their fears.
A snowman grins, his nose all wrong,
He forgot when the patch of dirt came along!

The Delicate Dance of Winter Light

The sun's a waltzer in a bright gown,
Spinning through clouds then falling down.
A snowflake prances, do you see?
A delicate dancer, wild and free.

Frosty whispers tickle the air,
A giggling pine tree stands, debonair.
As shadows stretch their chilly arms,
The world unveils its frosty charms!

A Reverie in Frosted Stillness

In a world where snooze buttons reign,
Pajamas dance in the cloud-stuffed lane.
Hot cocoa giggles in cozy mugs,
Marshmallows plotting some playful bugs.

The silence vibrates with laughter inside,
Chasing warmth on a snowy ride.
Snowball fights become a big fuss,
While neighbors shout, 'Don't hit the bus!'

Slumbering Pines of Solitude

Pines in pajamas, a sight to behold,
They chatter and mumble, as stories unfold.
Snowflakes as pillows, all fluffy and nice,
They cozy up tight, sipping coffee with mice.

Squirrels wear earmuffs, escaping the chill,
They scamper and giggle, with mischief to spill.
A dance of the branches, a waltz in the night,
As pines shake their boughs, they're a comical sight.

Dreamscapes in Silver Light

Under the moon's beam, there's mischief afoot,
The creatures all gather for a wild hoot-hoot.
Bunnies in moonboots, and hedgehogs that glide,
A wintertime party, with snowmen inside.

They slide down the slopes on a toboggan's spree,
With a popcorn machine and cups of hot tea.
In pajamas of snowflakes, they giggle and play,
As starlight and laughter light up the gray.

The Enchantment of Stillness

In stillness, the trees wear their frostbitten gowns,
While critters in scarves spread their laughter around.
A turtle takes selfies, a penguin does flips,
As frosty as ice, they're a comedic script.

The world holds its breath in a soft, snowy haze,
While otters in mittens engage in their plays.
They glide on a pond, with a splash and a slide,
Chasing their tails, that they just cannot hide.

Whispered Secrets of the Cold

The chill has its secrets, like tales from the breeze,
Of snowmen who gossip behind frozen trees.
With carrots for noses, they plot on the way,
To prank all the squirrels and sneak a quick play.

A jolly old rabbit with eyes full of cheer,
Unraveling jokes that the thaw will endear.
With snowflakes as confetti, they dance and they twirl,
In the wintry realm, where laughter's a swirl.

Frosted Silence of the Night

In blankets thick, the world is dressed,
A squirrel sneezes, and we're all stressed.
The moon is chuckling, so round and bright,
While penguins practice a tango at night.

Snowflakes dance with comedic flair,
While rabbits hop, without a care.
The icicles sway like they're on a spree,
As I sip cocoa, feeling quite free.

Gentle Shivers of Twilight

A chill in the air, the owls hoot loud,
While dogs in sweaters prance, oh so proud.
A snowman grins, his buttons askew,
As kids in mittens launch snowballs at you.

The hot chocolate spills, but who really minds?
We all burst into laughter, tangled in binds.
Chasing frost fairies on frosty trails,
While wearing bizarre hats, we tell silly tales.

The Snow's Gentle Murmur

The snow whispers secrets, oh so sly,
While birds in hats take to the sky.
Three polar bears slide, just for a thrill,
Then trip on a branch, oh what a spill!

A snow globe shakes, full of tiny cheer,
As rabbits giggle, hopping near.
The air is crisp, a comedy set,
With chilly jokes we'll never forget.

A Time for Reflection in Chill

The frost-bitten windows mirror our glee,
As we reflect on last week's cup of tea.
A penguin slips, then gives a wink,
While I munch cookies, pondering sync.

The candles flicker, shadows conspire,
While my warm socks dance by the fire.
In this frosty frame, oh what a jest,
With laughter and warmth, we're truly blessed.

Embracing the Numbness of Night

The moon wears a goofy hat,
With stars that twinkle, oh so flat.
Snowflakes fall like random confetti,
While I slip on ice, feeling unsteady.

I dance with shadows, quite the thorn,
In a frostbitten suit, I feel reborn.
Penguins waddle, my style's so bold,
As I trip through the night, all snug and cold.

The Tranquility of Frozen Streams

The river's a mirror, reflecting my slip,
As I make a big splash, oh what a trip!
Fish in the ice roll their eyes in despair,
While I perform stunts with flair everywhere.

Skaters glide past on blades that impress,
While I flail like a novice, I must confess.
With a cannonball leap and a frosty grin,
I become the ice king, let the laughter begin!

Crystalline Thoughts in the Chill

My brain is a snow globe, shaken and bright,
With thoughts spinning round, what a silly sight!
Each idea's a snowman, melting away,
As I seek out some cocoa to brighten my day.

I jot down my dreams on a frosty breeze,
While squirrels laugh at my mismatched shoes with ease.
Snowed in with jokes that just never land,
I chuckle at chaos, it's out of hand!

A Frosty Breath on Winter's Skin

A frosty breath whispers through my hair,
As I chomp on a snowman, unaware!
The cold nips my nose, what a silly tease,
While I shiver and giggle with utmost freeze.

I wrap up in blankets, a swaddled burrito,
Cocoa in hand, wearing my warmest beat-o.
With laughter that bursts like the ice on a stream,
This chilly chaos feels like a dream!

The Gentle Touch of Ice

The trees wear coats of sparkling frost,
And squirrels slide down on branches lost.
Snowmen waddle, needing a snack,
As snowballs fly—the ultimate attack!

Penguins shuffle with a comical sway,
While carolers slip and swing in dismay.
The world looks lovely, but watch your step,
Or you'll find yourself doing an ice-themed pep!

Echoes of a Frozen Landscape

The lake's a mirror, it's perfect and clear,
But don't mistake it—stay off, my dear!
There's laughter in the hush of the snow,
As frost bites your nose and you move way too slow!

Footprints lead to a towering hill,
Where kids scream down, it's quite the thrill.
But one slip, one flop, who will they blame?
The snowman's grinning, it's all part of the game!

Softening the Harshness

The world's a canvas, splashed with white,
Where hot cocoa brings pure delight.
With marshmallows floating, like clouds above,
Each sip is a hug, tasty, and full of love!

The mailman's bundled but still brings cheer,
With packages marked 'Open me here!'
A snowflake tickles and lands on your nose,
Just when you think you're done with the woes!

Nature's Hush in Dreamy White

As night falls gently, the stars blink awake,
While laughter echoes, in the crispness—what a break!
Snowflakes dance waltzes, in perfect sync,
As everyone tries not to slip on the brink!

With pup in tow, we trudge through the drifts,
He thinks it's all treasure—oh, the gifts!
A tumble's a joy in this fluffy bliss,
Nature's giggle—who could resist?

The Still Heartbeat of Frost

The snowflakes dance in awkward spins,
As raindrops freeze and begin their sins.
A snowman stumbles, then takes a bow,
It seems even he has lost the wow.

The trees are draped in a blanc tableau,
While squirrels plot on how to steal the show.
A mitten flies like a bird in flight,
Caught in the wind on this frosty night.

The chilly air bites with a playful tease,
Making noses red like ripe, odd cheese.
With every snicker, the icicles chime,
In this frozen jest, we bide our time.

And here we laugh 'til our sides feel sore,
At comical slips and the cold's uproar.
For in the stillness of this nippy haze,
Laughter and joy are the stars of the phase.

Serenity Wrapped in Frost

A blanket of white covers the ground,
With frosty chuckles all around.
The rabbits hop with a wiggly glee,
While snowflakes whisper, "Is this us? Oui!"

Each snowdrift serves as a playful throne,
Where frosty figures can lounge alone.
A snowball fight begins with a shout,
Then laughter echoes as we tumble about.

The sun peeks out, like a shy little cat,
And the snowmen grin with a funny hat.
As icicles dangle and twinkle bright,
The world feels jolly, oh what a sight!

So let the chill invade our cheeks,
And laughter fill our frozen peaks.
In the serene hush where the funny lives,
We'll find joy that the coldest week gives.

Glimmers of Light on Snow

In a field of white, the sparkles gleam,
Where snowflakes shimmer like a dream.
Two children race down a hill they find,
With snow in their mittens, pesky and blind.

A dog rolls over, covered in fluff,
While a cat in the window says, "That's enough!"
The world is a canvas, painted so bright,
Full of giggles beneath the moonlight.

Each icy step is a slapstick show,
As we shuffle along, all yelps and whoa!
The chilly breeze seems to sing and wink,
While frost-kissed cheeks begin to blink.

As lanterns flicker like fireflies bold,
A snowy laugh story unfolds.
In this playful dance with the sparkling glow,
We lose ourselves in the magic of snow.

Enigmatic Silence Under Stars

Beneath the stars, the night is still,
Where snow covers all, even the hill.
A crunch underfoot sounds like a giggle,
Making our paths twist and wiggle.

The wind gives a shiver, just out of sight,
While snowmen plot to rule the night.
Even the moon has a cheeky grin,
Like it's in on the frosty din.

With each snowflake that twirls through the air,
We giggle at shadows that catch us unaware.
The trees hold their breath, can you hear the fun?
As whispers of winter dance one by one.

So here's to the night, cold yet so bright,
Where silence becomes a joyous flight.
In frosty realms where laughter spins,
The magic of joy is where it begins.

Leaves of Silence

Fallen leaves in a big pile,
Squirrels scatter, thinking they're on trial.
They leap and dive in a leafy fight,
While the birds gossip with all their might.

The sun peeks through, a tease so bright,
But chilly winds give them a fright.
Each gust whispers secrets so bold,
As if nature's laughing at the cold.

Branches of Ice

Branches adorned with frosty lace,
Birds wearing hats, looking out of place.
They chatter and squawk, a comical show,
As icicles dangle like trophies in a row.

A snowman tries to strike a pose,
But melts away as laughter grows.
Nature's jokes in the crisp, clear air,
Reminding us all, there's fun everywhere.

Enchanted in the Snow's Embrace.

Snowflakes falling in a dizzy twirl,
Making kids jump, dance and whirl.
They build a fort, a strategic plan,
But the dog decides he's the snowball man!

With every toss, there's laughter loud,
As he rolls in snow to make his crowd.
Hot cocoa waits with marshmallow cheer,
While joyful giggles echo near.

Silent Whispers of Frost

Frosty whispers greet each dawn,
As rabbits hop along the lawn.
They slide and tumble, what a sight,
In a frosted ballet, pure delight!

The world's a stage in sparkling white,
As snowmen wobble, a comical sight.
Each snowball fight, a sticky affair,
In the chill of the breeze, laughter fills the air.

The Stillness Beneath Snow

Beneath the blanket, life snoozes tight,
While the moon winks down, a cheeky light.
Squirrels are plotting their next snack raid,
While dreaming of nuts that nature has made.

In the stillness, a playful breeze,
Carries laughter through the frozen trees.
Nature's humor wrapped in frost's embrace,
Tickling our hearts in this chilly space.

Hibernation's Soft Embrace

Snug in blankets, we all dive,
Hot cocoa helps to keep us alive.
Socks that match? A total disgrace,
But who needs style in this cozy space?

The cat's a ninja, plotting with glee,
While squirrels outside act like they're free.
Chasing shadows, they leap and prance,
While I just wish for a frosty dance.

Outside it's cold, a snowy affair,
Inside the snack stash, the treasure I share.
With every bite, laughter ignites,
And in this cocoon, we hide from the nights.

Mute Conversations in the Cold

Snowflakes fall with silent grace,
As I dance with my own clumsy pace.
Froze my tongue, can't talk to the trees,
They just giggle in the frigid breeze.

The penguin waddles, looking quite sly,
With a suit on, it's ready to fly.
While I trip on ice, feet gone awry,
Maybe next winter, I'll learn to glide by.

The snowman sneezes, then falls apart,
And I just stare, holding my heart.
Silent chuckles echo around,
As icicles cheer, like a jolly sound.

A Canvas of White Whispers

The world dons white, a blank slate here,
Snow angels flapping, full of cheer.
Yet even they tumble, fall, and flop,
Trying to make a snowman crop.

With every flake, my nose turns red,
And thoughts of warmth dance in my head.
But outside I'm stuck, throwing snow,
Is this a workout? Who can know?

A snowball fight, the laughter ignites,
We aim for cheeks, not hearts, what delights!
But I missed and hit Mr. Dean,
Now he's launching back, oh what a scene!

Winter's Gentle Breath

Chilled air nips, the breath escapes,
Like frosty bubbles from funny shapes.
I giggle at my scarf, it's quite a sight,
A fashion faux pas, it's a cozy plight.

The wind whistles tunes through naked trees,
While I'm bundled up, feeling like cheese.
Every step crunches, a symphony,
Even snowmen join the boisterous spree.

Laughter echoes in this snowy realm,
As I try to drive, it's chaos at the helm.
Nature's smile can't help but tease,
As I slip and slide, on frozen breeze.

Veil of Ice and Stillness

The trees wear hats of frosty white,
On squirrels, winter's a merry fright.
They slide down slopes with giggles loud,
While rabbits hop in a snowball crowd.

Snowflakes dance like they've lost their way,
As penguins waddle in a clumsy ballet.
With every slip, they cackle with cheer,
Who knew cold could bring so much jeer?

The pond becomes a skating rink,
As ducks don skates, oh, what a stink!
They quack and glide, so full of glee,
While falling into a snowman spree.

A snowman's hat is much too big,
He tips and tumbles, and takes a dig.
The charm of ice brings a chilly cheer,
In frosty realms, we laugh, not fear.

Frosted Breath of Dawn

The dawn awakens with a giggle bright,
While breath becomes a cloud, a frosty sight.
Coffee cups cling, they shake and chatter,
As pastries dance on plates, what a clatter!

Pigeons puffed and fluffed in line,
Waddle through snow, downright divine.
They strut like kings on their frosty throne,
As they peck at crumbs, they claim their own.

The sun peeks out, is it trying to play?
With little rays that jump and sway.
"Hey there, Mr. Chill!" they laugh and tease,
"Tread lightly now, or we'll freeze your knees!"

A jogger stumbles with a yelp of glee,
"Is that a marathon or a comedy spree?"
With each slip and pratfall, he finds good cheer,
In frosted dawn, we draw near.

Moonlight on Crystal Waters

The moonlight's silver slips and slides,
On icy lakes where laughter resides.
Fish don sunglasses, napping in bliss,
While otters frolic, can't help but miss!

A family of ducks strike a pose so proud,
Flapping their wings in a wobbly crowd.
They quack in harmony, a clumsy tune,
As the moon chuckles, "You're quite the boon!"

The ice beneath, a mirror of fun,
Reflecting joy as they race, oh, run!
With every splash, a giggle anew,
The moonbeams join in for a silly view.

A beaver builds a lodge like a king,
But trips on a twig—oh, what a fling!
In frosty realms where laughter entwines,
We find our joy beneath the signs.

Stars Adrift in a Cold Embrace

Stars twinkle bright in a chilly dance,
While snowflakes twirl to give it a chance.
A comet swoops with a laugh and shout,
"Hey, don't forget to put the pants out!"

Snowmen meet under a starlit roof,
Trading secrets and a winter goof.
With carrot noses that wiggle in laughter,
They brainstorm plans for a snowman's after.

Once upon a night, a snowball fleet,
Waged a friendly fight, oh, what a feat!
Through flurries and giggles, they threw with glee,
While polar bears cheered from a nearby tree.

A northern owl hoots with mischief's delight,
"Let's have a snow-off; it'll be quite a sight!"
With starlit wishes above, they will soar,
In frosty dreams, they find humor galore.

Lullabies of the Long Night

Snowflakes dance in jolly flight,
They slip and trip in the pale moonlight.
A squirrel in a scarf, what a strange sight,
Chasing his tail, in giggles, delight.

Frosty breath like clouds escaping,
Hot cocoa swirls, no sign of faking.
With marshmallows plopping, joy is shaping,
While snowmen plot their own fun-making.

Icicles hang like party crowns,
They glisten and giggle, no time for frowns.
While penguins slide, and no one drowns,
Even the grouchy old man renowns!

The night whispers tales, so blunt yet bright,
Of fluffed-up cats and their noodle fight.
In playful dreams, we drift, just right,
Till morning comes, a cheeky sight.

Icy Veils of Dawn

A frozen lake, a skating dance,
With wobbly legs, we take our chance.
Falling like penguins, what a romance,
Laughter erupts; it's our sweet prance.

The sun peeks in with a cheeky grin,
As frostbit flowers shove snows in.
They bloomed in dreams; oh, let's begin,
To giggle at bushes, covered in thin.

The dawn laughs at the sleepy trees,
While squirrels share their nutty leases.
They chat in whispers, aren't they keys?
The air is crisp, curling like breeze.

Now tea with snowflakes, a morning brew,
Isn't it silly? Can this be true?
In frosty sweaters, we bid adieu,
To morning's laughter, fresh and new.

Echoes in the Frozen Air

A whispering joke among the pines,
As critters chuckle where sunlight shines.
The snowman tells tales with funny lines,
  Of how he dreams of sunshine pines.

The ice-cold breeze has a silly twist,
Its playful nudges, how could we resist?
Elk in sunglasses, the weather missed,
  Oh, how they chase a snowball fist!

A battle of snow, a fluffy war,
With giggling yelps, they gather more.
Together they leap and roll on the floor,
  Joyful chaos, a comedy score.

In frosty glades, where laughter grows,
The echoing fun draws a curious nose.
Even the shadows can't keep repose,
As jests in the snow become all it knows.

Tranquil Slumbers of the Earth

Beneath the blankets of cozy white,
The earth takes naps in pure delight.
While ducks on ice decide to fight,
Who gets to swim in the morning light?

The owls share giggles, soft and low,
Watching the rabbits put on a show.
With flapping wings and stomp-paced flow,
It's a dance-off with a rhythmic glow.

As pine cones tumble without a care,
The trees join in, their dance so rare.
With trembling laughter all everywhere,
The quiet slumbers become a fair.

In this frosty realm where smiles are found,
The earth hums tunes, a merry sound.
With every giggle, joy will abound,
In slumbering laughter, we are all crowned.

Frosty Caress of Morning Light

The sun peeks out with a hesitant grin,
While squirrels wear mittens, a comical spin.
Snowflakes waltz, no rhythm they find,
As puppies chase shadows, a giggly rewind.

Frost clings to branches, a tiara of ice,
The mailman slips, rather not so nice.
Hot cocoa steams, but so does my nose,
As I sip too fast, chaos ensues, I suppose!

Icicles dangle, like teeth in a grin,
I slip on a patch, then laugh 'til I'm thin.
Frogs in the pond wear their frosty best,
As I build a snowman; he laughs, what a jest!

The wind whispers softly, with a chuckle or two,
As snowballs are thrown, with giggles anew.
In this frosty scene, where silliness grows,
Even the chill claims it knows how to pose!

The Sigh of Silent Trees

The trees stand still, dressed in white fluff,
While squirrels debate, which branch is enough.
Whispers of breezes, soft chuckles they share,
As snowmen compete with their frosty flair.

Beneath heavy branches, a snow-laden laugh,
Icicles swing like a merry old staff.
A bird on a branch, taking bets on the fall,
While a wave of the wind answers nature's call.

Pine needles, they ruffle, make small pranks and tease,
As I trip on my boots, oh dear, where's my ease?
The woods, they giggle with every frozen breath,
Creating a chorus of life, even in death.

Laughter echoes softly, as shadows stand close,
Winter's charm finds a way to compose.
So let's dance with the trees in this frosty delight,
In a world full of giggles, all silly, yet bright!

Beneath a Blanket of Silence

A blanket drapes soft, the world in repose,
While penguins wear jackets, striking a pose.
Snowflakes are jesters, they twirl and they flip,
As I fall on my back, making snowmen on a trip.

The quiet is noisy, with laughter so sweet,
While rabbits play tag on their frosty retreat.
Tea with marshmallows, a sweet little prize,
As each sip melts frost from the nose to the eyes.

A snowball lands squarely, right on my hat,
And laughter erupts, just like that!
The birds are all laughing at my silly show,
While I wrestle my scarf, caught in the flow.

Distant hills shimmer, their white gowns aglow,
Winter holds court with a comedic flow.
In this mirthful silence, the world feels so grand,
As each chuckle resounds through this frosty land!

Echoes of a Crystal World

The wind plays a tune, on the ice-coated ground,
As laughter erupts, in each snowman around.
A cat in a coat prances joyfully near,
While I chase my hat, which has vanished, oh dear!

The snowflakes, like dancers, pirouette on cue,
While children make angels, in forms meant for two.
Puddles freeze quickly, inviting a slip,
As I find myself flipping, from my own frozen trip.

An owl calls out, so wise and profound,
Yet even it chuckles at the chaos I've found.
Snowball wars erupt, there's laughter and glee,
As I duck for cover behind a tall tree.

With each echo and giggle, winter's bright charm,
Wraps us in joy, as we dance and disarm.
In this crystal world, where fun never ends,
Every laugh is a treasure, and each moment, a friend!

Abode of the Frostbound Dream

A penguin slid across the ice,
He thought it would be nice.
But ended up with knees so sore,
Now he just lays there, wanting more.

The icicles hang like chandeliers,
Glistening dreams from frozen years.
Snowmen fashion bowler hats,
While they gossip about the cats.

A polar bear in stripes so bold,
Sips cocoa from a cup of gold.
He whispers tales, and icebergs laugh,
Oh, to have seen that silly calf!

The breeze has secrets in a pitch,
Whisking snowflakes, oh what a glitch!
They tickle noses, dance on cheeks,
And leave behind bizarre mystiques.

Treetops Adoring the Snowfall

The trees wear cloaks of fluffy white,
Shouting, 'Look at us, what a sight!'
While squirrels bury acorns galore,
They forget where they hid them before.

A woodpecker, quite out of tune,
Taps on branches like a cartoon.
Every beat seems to chime,
Creating rhythms, flowing slime.

The branches shake with buried giggles,
As frosty branches do their wiggles.
The birds all sing in hushed delight,
While rabbits hop, oh what a sight!

Above the world, the snowflakes fall,
Like nature's confetti, covering all.
Yet down below, the critters play,
While winter's mischief holds sway.

The Language of Falling Flakes

Snowflakes speak in whispers bright,
Falling soft, like feathers' flight.
They giggle as they touch the ground,
In a language, silly yet profound.

Each flake is different, that we know,
But who made choices? Guess the snow!
They twirl and swirl in the frosty air,
Sending messages everywhere.

A snowball fight? Now that's good fun,
Toss a flake and then you run!
Puffs of white fly to the sky,
Just like laughter, oh my, oh my!

With rosy cheeks and dancing feet,
Winter's game is quite the treat.
The flakes, they shout, 'Come join the dance!'
In the frosty air, we all prance!

Shadows in a Snow-Kissed Glade

In a glade where shadows play,
Snowflakes giggle all day.
They dance around on little toes,
In the spaces where winter glows.

Bouncing shadows, losing their way,
Chasing sunbeams, come what may.
Footprints lead to a hide-and-seek,
While the chilly breeze takes a sneak.

A hare decides to take a leap,
Into a pile, soft and deep.
With a face full of snow, he winks,
As the glade laughs, oh how it thinks!

The trees chuckle, their branches bend,
As nature plays, it has no end.
So bring your joy, and sing a song,
In the glade where shadows belong.

Stillness Upon the Frozen Lake

A penguin slipped with quite a flair,
Doing the tango in frigid air.
Frogs still croak, despite the chill,
Shouting, "Hey, this is a thrill!"

The ice is slick, oh what a show,
As skaters skate, they twirl and go.
With every glide, a giggle bursts,
Life's frosty fun, it never thirsts!

Sled dogs dressed like fashion stars,
Barking beats, they've got the bars.
Snowballs fly with laughter's tune,
Underneath a bright, jolly moon.

Icicles dangle, looking like spears,
"Is that your nose?" a kid appears.
"Just pluck it, we'll make snow cream!"
Together, they chuckle, a chilling dream!

Embracing the Quiet Cold

A squirrel dances, tail so high,
Wearing acorns, oh what a spy!
Chirping birds in sweaters snug,
All for a laugh, they give a shrug.

The frost that kisses every tree,
Turns all the branches into glee.
Two neighbors fight with snow-filled arms,
Not quite a war, just winter charms.

A jolly snowman greets the day,
With carrot nose and hat of gray.
But when the dog just takes a bite,
"Oh, there goes dinner!" — what a sight!

In every flake, a joke is spun,
Cold can't steal the warmth of fun.
So let us laugh as we behold,
These frosty days, a joy untold!

The Softness of Snowflakes Falling

Snowflakes flutter like tiny wings,
While snowmen whistle, trying to sing.
The ground is blank, a canvas wide,
Yet, here comes Fido, full of pride!

"Look at my tail, it's a snowplow!"
He digs and dives, oh, what a vow.
Snowballs made with "just my luck",
Thwack! A snowball hits a truck!

Children tumble in a frosty heap,
Spinning tales that never sleep.
A plucky cat carves through the white,
Mewling loudly, in delight!

Laughter dances, crisp in the air,
Cozy sweaters and hats they wear.
Every flake has a story to tell,
In the snowy world where we dwell!

Ethereal Moments of the Cold

Twinkling lights on icy branches,
A gnome does jig, surprising glances.
Hot cocoa spills as laughter replays,
Sipping joy through winter's maze.

The moon is bright, a big ol' face,
Staring down at this snowy place.
"Watch me jump!" someone shouts with glee,
While landing hard, they laugh, "Oh me!"

The chill brings jokes with every breeze,
Making snow angels with silly ease.
Hot potato in mittens worn,
Look out, we've got snow-tornadoes born!

As we toast to the frosty cheer,
Elves throw snowflakes, and we all cheer.
Let's embrace this season's quirk,
In its cold and playful work!

Cascades of Silent Snow

Flakes twirl like dancers, high in the air,
Snowballs are flying, but no one's a square.
Sleds zoom down hills, they gleefully race,
Even the penguins wear smiles on their face.

Hot cocoa spills over, just like my cheer,
Marshmallows laughing, they float without fear.
Frostbite! Oh wait, just an ice cube on toes,
But we keep on sledding, nobody knows.

Snowmen are strutting, with carrot-nosed pride,
They hold a soft party, come join the slide.
With snowflakes that glisten, like diamonds they track,
All bundled in laughter, and also a snack.

So gather your friends, let the fun come alive,
Building a fortress, who'll take a dive?
The white fluff surrounds us, we're lost in the glow,
Each moment's a giggle, in cascades of snow.

Calm Reflections in Winter's Break

Icicles hang like teeth on a grin,
Birds in their jackets, looking so thin.
Snow lays a blanket, all soft and white,
While my cat's scheming, in shadows of night.

A snow shovel juggles, a neighbor's on deck,
Tripping and slipping, oh the poor guy's a wreck!
Snowflakes with laughter tumble by my nose,
"Catch me!" they tease, while the winter wind blows.

Sipping my tea, I warm up my hands,
Outside, winter giggles, with snow-covered bands.
A donut-shaped snowman, round as can be,
Winks at the world, oh, how funny is he!

So laughter and shimmer finish the show,
In this frozen theatre, we dance to and fro.
For in this still moment, we share a delight,
While calm echoes softly, on this magical night.

Celestial Whispers in Snow

Look at the sky, as it starts to confide,
With snowflakes that tickle and giggles that glide.
Who needs a blanket? Just a flurry of fun,
When laughter is ringing, oh, let's all run!

A snowball tournament, teammates in gear,
At the noontime meeting, it's crystal clear.
The snowman's a referee, with a grin big and wide,
While we plot our next move, with marshmallow pride.

The hot soup's a cauldron, bubbling away,
As spoons have their own war, on this snowy day.
We twirl like the flakes as they float all around,
Each giggle a note, in this symphony found.

So let's raise our cups, and join in the songs,
In this snowy ballet where nobody's wrong.
Chasing the whispers that swirl through the air,
With celestial glee, we'll find magic somewhere.

Still Waters Beneath Ice

Ponds wear a coat, so thick and so nice,
Skaters slip dancing, in each twinkle of ice.
When falling, they giggle, it's part of the show,
"Let's make it a challenge!" we all yell in tow.

The moon hides its chuckle, beneath snowy beams,
While friends start to twirl, living out their dreams.
A rodent on skates? Oh dear, that's a sight,
As he skids in a waddle, oh what a fright!

Snow angels are practicing flapping their wings,
While snowflakes giggle, and play with the springs.
The trees are now covered, with sugar-like dust,
A sugar rush party? Oh yes, that's a must!

So gather 'round warmth, let the fun take its place,
As laughter and joy dance in every face.
For in stillness we find an enchanting delight,
With joy beneath ice, through the magical night.

Serene Paths Through Snowdrifts

In snowdrifts high, I trudge and toil,
My boots get stuck in icy spoil.
A squirrel giggles from a tree,
'You're quite the athlete, don't you see?'

The dog runs past, a blur of white,
Chasing snowflakes, pure delight.
He stops to sniff, I trip and fall,
End up face-first in a fluffy wall.

Snowmen wink with carrots stout,
One yells, 'Why don't you chill out?'
I grin back, with frost on my nose,
Slide like a penguin, everybody knows!

At dusk we dance, a waltz, a spin,
With frosty breath, we both just grin.
The stars come out to join our fun,
In quiet nights, we all have won.

Midnight's Frosty Embrace

A midnight stroll in crunchy snow,
I slip and slide, but down I go!
The moonlight laughs, a frosty cheer,
'You should see this, it's quite the year!'

The trees wear coats of sparkling ice,
I wonder if they'll take advice?
'No sliding here,' they seem to say,
'You'll catch a chill, go back, okay?'

A rabbit hops with bouncy flair,
It throws a snowball, I can only stare.
With each wee hit, I clean my eye,
And mutter softly, 'Oh, my, oh my!'

The whispers dance on chilly air,
As giggles crackle everywhere.
In frosty fun, we lose all time,
Midnight's embrace, a silly rhyme.

Songs of the Sleeping Woods

In the woods where quiet lies,
A bear snores low, beneath the skies.
'Is that a song?' I pause to hear,
The branches giggle, 'Shhh, it's near!'

A snowflake lands atop my nose,
A gentle tickle, my laughter flows.
The trees join in, a choral glee,
While squirrels jam out with a glee!

The owls hoot tunes, the rabbits hop,
A frosty rhythm that just won't stop.
I clap along, though feet are cold,
The magic winter tales unfold.

With each bright note, the silence fades,
These goofy woods in jolly cascades.
In this night's song, we all partake,
Sleeping woods, awake, for laughter's sake!

Glacial Harmonies at Dusk

As dusk sets in with shades of gray,
I trip on ice—I'm on display!
A penguin paths, I waddle too,
Who's laughing now? Well, not a few.

The breeze hums soft, a chill refrain,
While icicles jingle on the windowpane.
'Make no mistake, we're cool as ice,'
Chimes one old tree, 'And that's so nice!'

A snowman grins, his buttons bright,
'Come dance with me,' he says in light.
I twist and twirl in playful fun,
To glacial beats, my heart is won.

With playful dusk, we all unite,
In frosty joy, we share delight.
The laughter echoes through the trees,
Let's make some more, if you please!

The Muffled Symphony of Chill

The snowflakes dance, oh what a sight,
They twirl and swirl, like a funny kite.
My nose is red, my cheeks a glow,
I trip on ice, that's how I show!

The carolers sing, but no one hears,
Their tunes are muffled by frosty tears.
I laugh and slip, down goes my hat,
The snowman grins, he's seen all that!

With hot cocoa warming my frosty hands,
I watch the squirrels make snowflake bands.
They gather nuts, then slide on their tails,
All while telling their wintery tales!

So when the chill wraps around your bones,
Just giggle and dance on the icy stones.
A symphony of cold, with laughter near,
This frosty season, let's spread some cheer!

Slumbering Landscapes in White

The world wears white, in fluffy attire,
As I make snowballs, feeling the fire.
I throw one high, it seeks the sky,
But lands on my dog, oh me, oh my!

The trees are dressed in coats of snow,
They dip and sway, just for show.
I swear I saw a snowman wink,
Was it my eyes, or did he drink?

Kids giggle as they tumble around,
A chorus of laughter wraps all around.
They build a fort, a castle grand,
While snowflakes cover the entire land!

Even the night, with its silvery glow,
Invites us out for a dance in the snow.
With twirls and spins, we embrace the chill,
In slumbering landscapes, our hearts will thrill!

Songs of the Shivering Woods

In the woods, a sound so bizarre,
The trees start to shiver, oh how they spar!
A squirrel skates on a frozen stream,
Chasing his nuts, oh what a dream!

The snowmen hum with carrot noses,
They form a band, where everyone dozes.
With hats askew and buttons mismatched,
They sing off-key, but none are attached!

The owls hoot, trying to keep track,
Of all the critters that gather back.
But as they sway, they tip on their toes,
And tumble down, where no one knows!

So here's to songs of giggles and freeze,
In shivering woods, let's dance with ease.
For laughter echoes through every tree,
A whimsical winter, as funny as can be!

Stillness Wrapped in Silver

Stillness falls on the world so bright,
Wrapped in silver, a dazzling sight.
A cat chases snowflakes, what a show,
In a moment of chaos, he then skids low!

The air is crisp, the laughter clear,
As friends come together, spreading cheer.
We toss a snowball, a friendly fight,
Then burst into giggles, what pure delight!

With boots so big, we trudge on through,
Leaving footprints like we all do.
The trees stand tall, decorated in white,
Whispering secrets in the soft moonlight!

So let's embrace this stillness so rare,
With funny tales to fill the air.
In silver tones, our hearts unite,
As we dance in the glow of a frosty night!

Hushed Melodies of the Season

Snowflakes dance with goofy glee,
Flopping down as if to see.
Gloves are lost, hats blowing around,
Laughter echoes, joy is found.

Sipping cocoa, mustache of foam,
Slipping on ice, a frosty roam.
Snowmen grin with carrot noses,
While snowballs fly like garden hoses.

Penguins slide on icy schemes,
Chasing tails in frosty dreams.
Furry critters in fuzzy hats,
Play tag with snickers and with spats.

The sky's a soft and silly show,
Clouds tumble like they don't know.
Under this charm, winter's cheers,
Wrap us all in smiles, not fears.

Blankets of Soft Silence

Blankets spread on frosty ground,
Cats in boots are safely found.
Between the flakes, a snowball fight,
Cousins giggle with sheer delight.

Icicles form like silly spears,
Half the fun? Avoiding cheers!
My dad slips down with epic flair,
The laughter spills into cold air.

Time for sleds, but wait! Not yet,
The dog jumps high, without a threat.
Chasing tails in fluff and white,
His antics spark pure delight.

At night we build a fort of dreams,
With pillows piled, like crazy schemes.
The silliness of frosty nights,
Turn sleepy heads to snowy sights.

Frosted Dreams in Twilight

The world is wrapped in frosty threads,
Penguins march in silly dreads.
Hats and scarves are mixed and matched,
Fashion critics getting scratched.

Glowing lights on rooftops sway,
Glitches twinkle in their play.
Sneezy sneezes fill the air,
As snowflakes fall without a care.

Bouncing snowballs take a dive,
Chase the giggles, feel alive!
Huddled in a snowball heap,
Unicorns of fluff, we leap!

Shadows dancing amid the frost,
Mom's lost mitten, what a cost!
But grin and bear it, laugh out loud,
In this jolly, snowy crowd.

The Calm Before the Chill

We peek outside all bundled tight,
Snowmen plotted through the night.
Kittens prance on clumps of snow,
While puppies dig, and chaos flows.

Chimneys puff while we will sip,
Last cookie bites at every trip.
Giggles squashed beneath the ice,
Slick turns that are not very nice.

The sleds await, our laughter sings,
Silly falls, oh look—more flings!
Snowflakes teasing from the sky,
As we tumble, roll, and fly.

A toast to all the joyful woes,
In transient warmth where laughter glows.
Between the flakes, we've found a thrill,
In the calm, let's chase the chill!

The Whisper of a Snowy Evening

The flakes fall down with a gentle pout,
Each one makes me yawn, what's this about?
A snowball fight? I only wish to nap,
But here comes a snowman on my neighbor's lap!

His carrot nose is slightly askew,
I laugh so hard, I spill my stew.
The snowman waves, what a silly sight,
He's wearing my scarf, oh what a fright!

I've built a castle, it's fit for a king,
But wait, my dog's now wearing a wing!
He prances about, a snowy ballet,
Who knew he could dance in such a frosty way?

Giggles erupt from the children at play,
As they each take a tumble, slip and sway.
They build and they launch with gleeful shouts,
All while I sip cocoa, avoiding the route!

Muffled Footsteps in the Night

I tiptoe outside, the world dressed in white,
Each step is a squish, what a silly plight!
The neighbors peek out, are they spying on me?
Or just jealous of my wild snow-burrito spree?

Snowflakes land on my nose, what a surprise,
Now I'm a snowman with sparkly eyes!
I frolic and roll, feeling quite spry,
Until I get stuck and let out a cry!

A voice calls to me, 'What are you doing?'
'Trying to be festive, and maybe moonuluing!'
Laughter erupts in the frosty air,
As I wiggle and jiggle, in a fluff ball of flair!

I see shapes in the shadows, are they bears?
Nope, just my friends in extravagant layers!
Together we snowball, hearts full of mirth,
Under the gleaming stars, oh what a birth!

Shadows Cast by the Pale Moon

Under the glow of the moon's chilling light,
My shadow dances, oh what a sight!
It swaggers and wiggles, with glee it does prance,
As I stomp through the snow, in a clumsy romance.

My shadow grabs snowballs, and goes for the throw,
It tickles my sides with a playful glow.
I chase after laughter, echoing bright,
While tripping on ice in the middle of night.

The moon chuckles softly at my silly show,
As snowmen conspirators plot down below.
They're whispering secrets, oh what could they mean?
Could it be that they're joining my frosty scene?

A race through the flakes, off into the dark,
We laugh and we giggle, igniting a spark.
Though shadows may vanish with the break of dawn,
Our memories will linger, this fun will live on!

Glacial Breezes of Serenity

With a gust of wind, my hat takes flight,
As I run like a goose, oh what a sight!
Chasing it down on my slippery feet,
While icicles laugh at my cold little beat.

The yard is a sea of sparkles and dreams,
Where sleds fly like rockets, or so it seems.
I take one ride, oh the speed is absurd,
Until I hit snow, no graceful maneuver!

While I lay there stunned in the fluffy white fluff,
The snowmen all cackle, enough is just enough!
But whoops, here comes Fido, with a leap and a bound,
Not realizing he's made himself quite the mound!

So here we are, in our wintery cheer,
With laughter and joy, let's raise a cold beer!
Glacial breezes blow softly tonight,
As we relish this madness, oh what a delight!

Beneath a Shroud of White

The snowflakes dance with such a flair,
A flurry of fun, beyond compare.
Sleds zoom by while giggles ring,
As winter's chill wears a cozy bling.

Snowmen stand, looking quite grand,
With carrot noses, they take a stand.
But oh dear friend, what's that surprise?
A squirrel in red gloves, oh my, how it tries!

Hot cocoa spills, and marshmallows fly,
Accidental battles, oh me, oh my!
The joy of the frost, it warms our souls,
Laughter erupts, as the fun unrolls.

Under the clouds that seem to pout,
We chase after joy, there's never a doubt.
In the blanket of white, we frolic and play,
This chilly adventure brightens the day.

The Pause of Nature's Breath

Trees wear coats of crystal sheen,
While squirrels plot mischief, unseen.
A breath of cold, nature's lull,
As dogs chase their tails, in an endless pull.

Birds in hats appear so grand,
Chirping tales of frost and land.
Snowball fights break out with glee,
Who knew the snow could set us free?

Icicles hang like swords of glee,
Threatening to fall, watch out, oh me!
Each puff of breath a cloud so white,
Comedy unfolds in this frosty light.

Laughter echoes through the trees,
As children tumble—oh, what a tease!
In nature's pause, we find our cheer,
Winter's fun, let's give a cheer!

Crystal Quietude

In the hush of frost, we gather round,
With snowflakes twirling, laughter's the sound.
A bunny in boots hops, don't you see?
There's humor in nature, wild and free.

The moon grins down on a glittering quilt,
While whispers of snow create a slick tilt.
Hot soup spills as we clumsily dance,
Who knew winter held such a chance?

Pine trees wear snow like a fancy hat,
As cats join the game, don't fall, oh brat!
We slide on the ice, a comical joy,
Forget shiny toys; we've found the ploy!

The chilly breeze carries giggles so bright,
Under the stars, everything feels right.
In the crystal calm, we play without fears,
Finding laughter and warmth in the chilly years.

Frosted Footprints in Time

Heed not the chill, it's a time of cheer,
With frosted footprints, let's give a cheer!
Each step we take leaves a funny tale,
As ice beneath us begins to pale.

Snow plows rumble, a noisy affair,
As we dodge their paths, unaware of the glare.
A dash here, a slide, oh what a twist,
Who knew that falling could feel like bliss?

With every tumble, we roar with delight,
As giggles erupt, what a funny sight!
We build our dreams in the fluff and white,
In frost we trust, as day turns to night.

Covered in snow, our worries now fade,
As laughter fills the air and fun's on parade.
These frosted footprints, a story to share,
In the heart of the chill, we find joy laid bare.

Milton Keynes UK
Ingram Content Group UK Ltd.
UKHW021950151124
451186UK00007B/172